NORTHERN CROSSWAY

- a 196 mile coast to coast walk from Arnside to Bamburgh

Allan Brackenbury

Published by Linda Brackenbury, 127 Glandon Drive,
Cheadle Hulme, Cheadle, Cheshire SK8 7HD

First edition

Printed by Deanprint Ltd., Cheadle Heath Works, Stockport Rd, Stockport SK3 0PR

Whilst every effort has been made to ensure that the information in this book is correct, the author or the publisher can accept no responsibility for errors, loss or injury however caused.

The map sketches in this book are intended as a rough guide only and should not be used for navigational purposes.

Dedicated to George and Jeanne, Liz and Keith, my first companions along the Northern Crossway

Brackwalks

http://www.brackwalks.co.uk

ISBN: 978-0-9931833-1-7
A catalogue record of this book is available from the British Library

CONTENTS

INTRODUCTION   1

THE WALK

Introduction

This walk originated in 1982. Our group of friends had enjoyed Long-Distance walking together. We had followed the Pennine Way, the Offa's Dyke Path, and the Coast to Coast Walk, and we wanted to tackle something similar. But we didn't fancy a coastal path, and all other long-distance walks that we knew about were either too tame or too short. We wanted a route that would take about a fortnight, passing through majestic countryside and giving us some worthwhile (but not dangerous) hill climbs. So I devised this route, from the west coast at Arnside, going roughly north-east to the east coast at Bamburgh, providing us with a memorable walk through wonderful scenery.

Most of the route is in Cumbria and Northumberland, with about two days in Durham and a few minutes of the first day in Lancashire. What is now Cumbria used to be Westmorland before the 1974 boundary revisions apart from the Sedbergh area which was in the West Riding of Yorkshire. This explains why the route passes through a corner of the Yorkshire Dales National Park, - as well as the Northumberland National Park. The Northern Crossway spends a day in the Howgill Fells and two days in the Cheviots. Other highlights include Middleton Fell, High Cup Nick, the Harwood valley, Blanchland and its surrounding moorland, and the towns of Appleby and Hexham. For the four days in areas where the route is potentially hazardous in bad weather, low level alternatives are given.

I believe that the entire route uses public rights of way or other land where walkers have traditionally been allowed access. Occasionally the path on the ground differs from the way shown on the map: this guide follows the visible path. I am assuming that people who walk the Northern Crossway will take Ordnance Survey Explorer or Outdoor Leisure 1:25000 maps, and know how to read them. Consequently the maps in this book are only sketches, and I have not given long descriptions where the route of the path is obvious.

We first did this walk in 1982. Since then I have followed the complete route three times and visited parts of it on many other occasions making revisions as necessary. It is gratifying that some paths that were so blocked thirty years ago that they could not be used, are now fully open, with stiles and waymarks. But there is still room for improvement as some rights of way remain unfit for use, notably in Harwood Forest.

Between Dufton and Langdon Beck the Northern Crossway uses the same tracks as the Pennine Way. This is deliberate, because the scenery here is so wonderful, - and because there are few other ways for walkers across the Pennines. Elsewhere parts of the NC route are shared with other `official' Trails, but these are coincidental, as the NC was planned before the other routes appeared on the scene.

It had been my intention to write a guide soon after our trek in 1982, but I realised that the project needed far more time than I could spare. But on walking the route again after retirement, I felt inspired once more to write a simple guide to the Northern Crossway. It is a route that I have enjoyed walking, and I hope that others will enjoy it also.

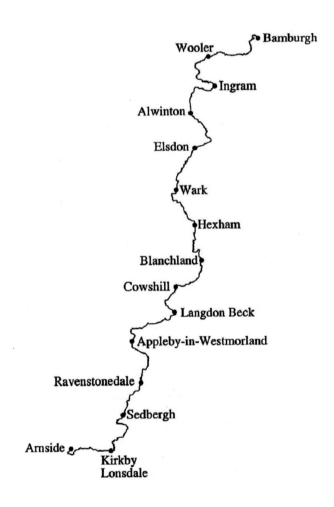

STAGE 1: ARNSIDE to KIRKBY LONSDALE

Distance 14.5miles/23.2kms
Ascent 1870ft/575m

1:25,000 Maps
Outdoor Leisure 7 - SE Lakes
Outdoor Leisure 2 - S & W Yorkshire Dales

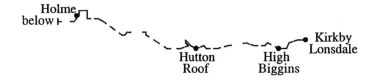

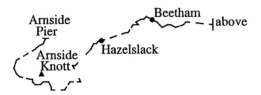

The Northern Crossway commences at Arnside, a small resort on the tidal River Kent, on the final stage of its journey to the sea. Until the railway came in 1857, it was an insignificant riverside village. Eventually the railway was to bring visitors, but it had a more immediate effect as the viaduct caused the river estuary to silt. Milnthorpe port lost its trade, so the railway company built Arnside pier and the road to Sandside as partial compensation. But the estuary silted further and the pier's use by commercial traffic lasted less than fifty years. It is still in regular use by fishermen and sightseers and it makes an ideal starting point for the Northern Crossway.

The first day's walk passes through four distinct scenic areas. The first and longest, - and most memorable, - is the Area of Outstanding Natural Beauty between Arnside and Beetham. It is well wooded, undulating, - and interesting. There is a short optional addition to the walk, to the top of Arnside Knott. This is an excellent vantage point, and the climb comes early in the day when walkers are fresh and eager, but you need to judge whether the half-hour taken here will be needed later in the day. The second area is a series of pasture fields between the A6 and M6. Then comes the third area, along a long path through a remote limestone region between Holmepark Fell and Hutton Roof Crags, with hardly a house in sight. The final area is a gentle climb through sheep fields between Hutton Roof and Kirkby Lonsdale.

The general direction of the Northern Crossway from west coast to east coast is north-east, but it commences paradoxically by following the coastline south-westerly. The walk starts at Arnside Pier (SD 456788) and follows the Kent Estuary along the promenade (or along the beach at low tide). When the road ends, continue on the paved path beside the Kent past the coastguard's office for about 3/4 mile. (At exceptional high tides the lower part of the coastal path is flooded. In these circumstances turn left before the coastguard's cabin, up a tarmac path signed 'Knott Road, Silverdale' to a road above. Turn right and keep to the major road at each junction until it narrows and descends to the kissing gate at New Barns.)

At New Barns Bay the path turns inland to join a rough lane just as it crosses a stream (444777). Turn left along this lane and leave it shortly through a kissing gate signed 'Public Footpath to Arnside Knott and Silverdale'. Follow the path across a meadow into a wood. Continue on a clear wide ascending track, ignoring side tracks on both left and right. After a short stretch in the open the wood resumes and the NC veers left alongside a wall and soon meets a bridleway at a T-junction (451772). Turn right, signed 'Arnside Tower'. After about 1/4 mile there is a crossing of major paths. The signed path on the left is an optional addition to today's walk: it goes to the summit of Arnside Knott (522ft). Memorable views of Lake District mountains and coastal scenery justify the half mile climb. Return the same way.

Continue on the bridleway to Arnside Tower, ignoring side paths, to meet a road at 457772. Take the lane opposite, to Arnside Tower farm. Pass right of the farm to reach the Tower, a 15th century pele tower, built as a sanctuary at times of raids by Scots. It is now unsafe. Descend left to join an eastward path signed to 'Middlebarrow and Blackdyke', which soon enters a wood. Follow this path along the edge of the wood for a long half mile and then turn left onto a path signposted to 'Blackdyke' which leaves the wood, then runs beside the railway for a further half mile. The Tower and Knott can be seen on the left. Turn right on a concrete track under the railway into a big field. When the concrete ends, continue along the track up a slight rise, but then veer right, aiming for a grey house on a minor road (472783). Turn right here, then just after Carr Bank Road turn left on a path. Follow the trodden route for 1/4 mile until you reach two stone stiles in a wall. Take the right hand one and go forward to join a good gravel track to a minor road at Hazelslack where there is another pele tower.

Turn right and soon reach a T-junction. Here continue straight ahead, on a footpath signed 'Beetham via Fairy Steps'. Follow the farm track to a gate into Underlaid Wood. The path climbs steadily through the wood. At one point it goes left then turns right and narrows to ascend a modest cliff by stone steps. At the top it goes left, then resumes its previous direction. This is just a prelude to the Fairy Steps (487789), where the path becomes extremely narrow, rising left in a cleft in a much taller limestone wall. The way looks such a squeeze that walkers will have to use hands as well as feet to ascend and will probably need to pass rucksacks up separately. In the days before Arnside had its own church or road to the outside world, villagers used this route to go to church in Beetham. They must have been slim in those days! Walkers who feel unable to pass through the cleft can follow a gentler signed concessionary route.

The top of the Fairy Steps is a good viewpoint. Arnside Knott, estuary and viaduct are visible for the last time today, (although in good weather they can be seen on the next two days) and you begin to realise that you are starting to travel somewhere. There are several paths here. The NC goes north-easterly (left of straight on) through woodland on a wide waymarked path marked by a tree with a curious left hand bend in its trunk. After about a quarter mile ignore a left track opposite a gate on the right. Then at a footpath crossing marked by a little cairn go straight on, following a wide forest track which immediately veers off to the right. After about 300 paces look out for a waymarked path off on the left and take this, soon forking left by a mossy wall. It eventually descends, past a ruined cottage, out of the wood into a field which exits onto a road at 494796. Turn right into the attractive village of Beetham. This has a tea room/shop, an inn and a bus route.

The NC route in Beetham passes the church and shop, turns right at the 'Wheatsheaf' corner, then immediately goes left to meet the A6 by the village school. Continue along the A6 for a short distance, then turn left along a farm road at 501792. Pass left of the farm outbuildings, then continue eastward, soon gently rising through the centre of a field. In the next field go half left, aiming to the right of Pye's Bridge Farm. Go through a gate onto a lane. Here turn left, cross over Holme Beck, and then turn off right on a footpath signed 'Holme'. This resumes the eastward route, mainly along field boundaries, crossing the main railway line by an imposing footbridge, then continuing beyond the B6384. Just before Holme the path diverts left, then passes between houses to emerge on the village road. (Holme is 5 minutes away on the right. It possesses an inn, shop, post office and bus route. This is your last chance of refreshments before Kirkby Lonsdale.) Turn left for a short distance, then ascend Park Lane on the right. This leads to the peaceful Lancaster Canal, the only canal seen on the Northern Crossway, and then only for 1/4 mile. This part of the canal is in good condition but it is long out of use. Turn left along the towpath to the road that crosses on the level at 527797. If canal navigation is to be restored, this is one of the roads that will need to be raised. Turn right along this road, pass under the M6, then turn right for a short distance along the narrow and busy A6070.

Beyond Holme Park Farm (530794) turn left along the clear track that rises into the limestone hills for about a mile and becomes a most attractive grassy path. It has hedges on both sides at first, then just on the right. Ignore side tracks off on the left. Eventually at a junction of paths, fork right. Very soon, after a gate (543788) the path turns left, climbing in open hillside, leaving the wall and woodland behind. Soon it forks: bear right and cross two walls with gates. After crossing a farm track the path veers right to cross a road at 552789. This road marks a change in the route's character. Around Holmepark Fell the path has been in a secluded hillside with few landmarks, making navigation potentially difficult. But beyond the road, after a slight climb up the northern edge of Hutton Roof Crags, the path levels off along a heathland ridge, providing wonderful views on the left. The hills on the east side of the River Lune are prominent including Barbon Fell and Middleton Fell. Later on Ingleborough can be seen further south. Eventually the path descends: at a path junction by a large crag face, turn left and immediately fork right, dropping steeply into Hutton Roof village (571783).

Turn left in Hutton Roof and then immediately right along Gallowber Lane. Cross a stream, then take a signed path on the right. It starts as a green lane between walls, then climbs through several large pasture fields and the route is not always clear on the ground. However a line of telegraph poles is a good guide to follow as the track is close to this line on the journey upward, then down and up again. The path then crosses a wall above Longfield Barn (a ruin) and continues, following the foundations of a former wall. In the next field go half left to a stile in the far corner which leads to a further field. Keep in the same direction to a stile which emerges onto Pit Lane at 597785. Turn right along it into High Biggins and when the road turns right (602783), continue straight on through a kissing gate on a short path to Low Biggins. Turn left, cross the busy A65 road, and continue ahead. Opposite Abbot Hall Farm turn right along New Road past the fire station to reach Kirkby Lonsdale's market square.

STAGE 2: KIRKBY LONSDALE to SEDBERGH

Distance 15.8miles/25.3kms
Ascent 2480ft/763m

1:25,000 Maps
Outdoor Leisure 2 - S & W Yorkshire Dales
Outdoor Leisure 19 - Howgill Fells

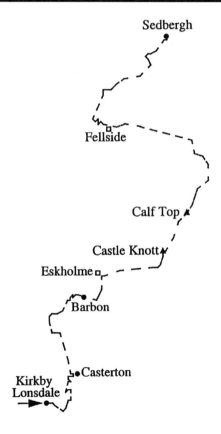

Today's walk is dominated by the ascent of Middleton Fell, a long expanse of unfenced hillside, providing an excellent walk with magnificent views. Additionally, there is good walking countryside before and after Middleton Fell, with the added bonus of Howgill Fell views on the approach to Sedbergh. There is also a 'Bad Weather' route that stays in the valley, for use when weather conditions make it inadvisable for walkers to be out on the open fell.

Leave Kirkby Lonsdale market square on the south side, along Jingling Lane, past the toilets. When the lane ends turn right along a paved footpath which leads to the old main road. Turn left and cross the River Lune by Devil's Bridge, a magnificent mediaeval structure, now closed to cars. Continue ahead across the A683 onto a lane, soon forking left uphill. Beyond a caravan site turn left along a narrow bridleway between hedges, named Laitha Lane on the map and Colliers Lane on the signpost. At a T-junction go left beside Casterton Golf Course and reach the A683 near a former toll cottage. Turn left on the busy road which is twisting and lacks a pavement, but not for long. At 620790 take a kissing gate on the right into a long thin field. Go right with Casterton Hall visible ahead. When you reach its entrance drive turn right for a short distance then go sharp left along the lane to Mill Hill House (620795). Here take a right footpath, round the edge of a wood. Just after passing buildings above on the right, turn left over a stream and through a wood followed by a field and then another wood. The path continues in fields over a wobbly ladder stile then beside walls and fences to meet Lowfields Lane at 617812.

Here turn left and pass under the drive to Underley Hall. Continue north and cross Barbon Beck by Beckfoot Farm (614818). Normally there is no problem in using the ford here, but there is a delightful packhorse bridge nearby, for use when the river is too deep or swift. Turn right, following the beck and keeping on the north side of it for half a mile to the A683. The path crosses Kirkby Lonsdale golf course. Four bridges over the beck have been provided for golfers: in contrast, near the main road an ancient bridleway from Kendal is crossed and this fords the stream. Further west this bridleway also fords the River Lune and unsurprisingly it is not often used today.

On reaching the A683 (623825) turn right over the beck, then immediately go left guided by the "Main road to Barbon" stone. Barbon has a shop (turn right at the war memorial) and an inn. Until 1954 it had a railway station, and the line continued in use for goods traffic until 1966. The level crossing was just before the church and the station was on the right. Modern housing has obliterated most of its traces. Yet this line could so easily have become a trunk route into Scotland, still open today. Inter-company rivalry caused the Settle-Carlisle railway to be built, so that became the main line and the route through Barbon and Sedbergh lost its importance.

Continue straight through Barbon village. Just beyond the parish church turn left on a metalled lane which crosses the beck. It then climbs and curves sharply to the right.

At this point (632826) leave it along a path which goes north along the east side of Ellers wood and continues through a field to approach a farm (Eskholme) at 634833. Here turn right and climb steeply up to a gate. Beyond the gate is open hillside. Now commences the major ascent of the day. At first it is pretty tough, but it gets easier higher up (or maybe walkers have got used to the gradient by then). There is a clear grassy track to follow, ascending Thorn Moor, slightly north of the route shown on the map. After a long long mile and a half it reaches a cairn which marks Castle Knott at 1759ft, the first major summit on the fell.

Continue on the path, descending then rising to the trig point which marks Calf Top, the highest point of Middleton Fell, 1999ft. A wall on the right joins the path shortly before the summit and keeps it company for a long time afterwards. It marks the boundary of the Yorkshire Dales National Park. From your vantage point there are fine views across steep sided Barbon Dale and green Dentdale. On a clear day Arnside can be seen as well as the coast and many hills of the Lake District, Howgills, and Yorkshire. From Calf Top a good path continues along the ridge, not losing much height initially. Eventually it starts a gradual descent, and swings round anticlockwise, continuing for 2 miles to the farm at Fellside (636889). Then the farm's zig zag access lane is followed down to the A683 at 630890. Wide grassy spaces allow walkers to take some short cuts; in particular there is a cut-off to the right just before the main road.

Turn right on the A683 but not for long! Where it turns left, continue straight on along Jordan Lane. This is a narrow metalled road with grass in the middle, between high hedges. It follows the route of the Roman Road from Ribchester to Low Borrow Bridge near Tebay. After half a mile, just as the lane turns left under the former railway line, turn right on a signed bridleway (635902) which at first is hard to find. Follow the left hand wall for a very short distance until it turns left, then go diagonally left down a small bank to join an overgrown track lying between remnants of two broken down walls. Before long the track becomes clearer, and it emerges into a field. Follow a left hand wall, then continue ahead, meeting an unfenced lane. Turn right along this lane and soon fork left, down to Abbot Holme. This is a delightful approach to Sedbergh, with the town peeping through the trees and the broad expanse of the Howgill Fells rising beyond.

Cross the River Dee by the narrow bridge at Abbot Holme, then take the first footpath on the left, climbing across a golf course, to a narrow gate in a wall. Turn left to meet the River Rawthey and then go right, descending to a footbridge (651913), which is stronger than it looks. Cross the river and turn right along a lane through Birks hamlet to Birks House. Take the path going round the side and rear of the house, leading into a lane between sports fields. Cross a road by kissing gates, onto a grassy path in a field. This becomes tarmac after another kissing gate. On the right is a school playing field. Where this ends the path turns right, still beside the playing field. Then turn left beside the church to reach Main Street in the centre of Sedbergh (657921). Turn right for the Tourist Information Centre (659922), currently titled Dales & Lakes Book Centre.

Low Level/Bad Weather Route Kirkby Lonsdale to Sedbergh

The main route is followed as far as Beckfoot Farm, by the ford and packhorse bridge across Barbon Beck (614818). It is rejoined where Jordan Lane leaves the A683 (631891).

Go forward through Beckfoot Farm along High Beckfoot Lane which soon becomes a green path between walls. At a path junction keep straight on, rising through an apparent tunnel of trees. The way skirts the golf course and continues as a narrow green path between hedges. Black Beck is crossed by a ford; if this is too deep to walk through, go into the field on the right and use the bridge. Pass right of Treasonfield and follow its tarmac drive to the A683 at 621837.

The next two miles are spent along tarmac lanes little wider than a farm cart. They are unexciting to walk along, but they provide good views, and some wild raspberries at the roadside. On arrival at the A683 turn left and immediately right onto Betweengates Lane. Turn left at a T-junction and soon afterwards fork left (626849). The lane continues generally north to meet the A683 again at Middleton Hall Bridge (625874). Here take a bridleway on the left, diagonally through a field to a gate. The path continues north beside a hedge for two fields, then becomes a farm track which bridges a stream and goes on to Low Waterside Farm. Go left here between the River Lune and the farm buildings. Leave the riverside beyond the farm and follow a fence on the right. After a stone barn the path turns right, then left through a wood. Briefly it meets the Lune again, then climbs to rejoin the A683 at a blind corner. Cross the road with care, turn right for a few yards, then left along Jordan Lane, rejoining the main route.

STAGE 3: SEDBERGH to RAVENSTONEDALE

Distance 10miles/16kms
Ascent 3200ft/985m

1:25,000 Maps
Outdoor Leisure 19 - Howgill Fells

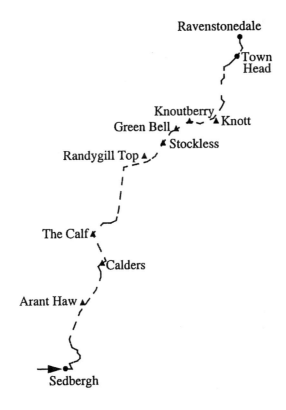

This is one of the finest stretches of the Northern Crossway. All day is spent in the Howgill Fells, alluring rounded hills with hardly a fence, tree, or building in sight. A few of the climbs are steep, but they are well worth doing. However, unless you are an expert navigator, you should not tackle this route in mist. Even in good weather, route finding needs care because there are many valleys and few landmarks. Additionally, there are numerous tracks in the Howgills and these do not always coincide with paths marked on the map. There is an alternative low level route to use in bad weather, and this is described after the main route. If conditions should deteriorate when you are out on the fells, there is an escape route along Bowderdale.

From the Tourist Information Centre in the middle of Sedbergh, take Joss Lane upward past the toilets and car park, and bear right. At 661924 the lane becomes a clear footpath, rising steadily beside a stream, Settlebeck Gill. Keep to the path as it continues upwards, sometimes close to the beck and sometimes distant. Eventually the path climbs higher than the stream and meets a clear bridleway on a ridge (661941).

Follow this bridleway upward to the right. Soon a clear path leaves on the left to ascend Arant Haw (1989ft) and then it returns to the main bridleway. Either path can be taken: many walkers will want to bag the summit, but others will think that there is already enough climbing to do today, and an extra one is more like punishment than enjoyment. The two routes rejoin at Rowantree Grains, a striking viewpoint. It is a col with majestic folds of the mountains left and right into valleys far below. The path descends along the ridge, then climbs sharply to the summit of Calders (2213ft), marked by a cairn.

It is not far from Calders to The Calf, the highest point on the Howgill Fells (2220ft). There is a broad stony track north-westward from Calders to the trig point on The Calf. On a clear day there are magnificent views in all directions, back to Arnside and the coast, forward to the Pennine chain, and also including fells of the Lake District and Yorkshire. Nearer are Wild Boar Fell, Yarlside, and the deep valleys of the Howgills.

From The Calf, the stony track turns east. It is still clear but narrower and at first it is fairly level. At two path junctions close together, fork right both times. Then the path descends and veers north into Bowderdale, a long, remote, and peaceful valley. It is tempting to remain in Bowderdale, and indeed walkers can continue in the valley for an extra 3 miles. But there are a further 3 miles to walk, in less beguiling scenery, to reach Ravenstonedale. This route is recommended for use if conditions inhibit the NC's climb out of Bowderdale.

The toughest part of the day's walk occurs on leaving Bowderdale, a climb of 800 feet up Randygill Top. Some 2 miles beyond The Calf, at around 679996 Bowderdale

Beck is joined by Hazel Gill from the west and Randy Gill on the east. Cross Bowderdale Beck with care and get onto the north side of Randy Gill. Randygill Top is now before you. Follow the visible upward path for half an hour or so to the summit (2047ft) which is marked by a modest cairn. From here take a good path north eastwards over Stockless (694006) to the top of Green Bell (1985ft). Its trig point is a good landmark.

It is practically all downhill from now on and there are paths all the way from Green Bell to Ravenstonedale. However, they may not be clear on a misty day so some compass work may be necessary. Continue north-eastwards on the visible track that soon drops steeply, then rises to Knoutberry (704013). Fork right on the approach to Knoutberry's summit, and keep on along a grassy path, descending gently. Take a path round the west side of Knott. Pass on the east and north sides of a walled enclosure containing a meagre copse of trees and a ruined building, named Thornthwaite (716021). Continue ahead on Thornthwaite's access track. Walls close in at Wye Garth and soon you reach Kilnmire (719034), the first farm met since Sedbergh. Take the farm drive to reach a minor road at Town Head (722036).

This is the start of Ravenstonedale, an interesting spread out village that shows signs of former importance. Follow the road through the village to the Black Swan Inn. There is also a shop and other accommodation.

Low Level/Bad Weather Route Sedbergh to Ravenstonedale

This route is a fine walk in its own right. It keeps east of the Howgill Fells, following good tracks in valleys as far as possible. Even so, it reaches a height of 1326 feet, on the road near Adamthwaite. It only coincides with the main route as Ravenstonedale village is approached.

From the Tourist Information Centre in Sedbergh follow the main road eastwards. At a fork beyond the fire station go right along the A684 as far as the narrow bridge over the River Rawthey. Do not cross the river: instead turn left on the footpath which runs alongside its north bank. Soon after crossing A683 main road the path leaves the river, rises, and passes through Buck Bank farmyard to meet a lane (678928). Turn right past Thursgill farm (681934) where the tarmac ends and continue on a farm track as far as Fawcett Bank (685940), the limit for vehicles. Rounded summits of lesser Howgill fells appear above on the left, and there are good views ahead and across the Rawthey Valley.

At Fawcett Bank the route turns slightly left, then resumes as a green lane at the left side of a field. It continues as a well trodden footpath running parallel to the Rawthey and the A683, boggy at times, some times close to a wall or fence, some times in open fellside with the gorse and bracken, and crossing several tributary streams. Eventually the Cautley Holme Beck, a significant tributary with its own side valley, is crossed by a footbridge (693968). There is a fine view along the valley to the steep sided hills, and Cautley Spout waterfall. Meet the wide stony valley path and turn right to return to the Rawthey.

Here there is a dilemma. The NC continues along a bridleway which used to cross the Backside Beck by a footbridge. This bridge has gone and the bridleway has been diverted to cross the beck by a ford at 700975 and in most weather conditions walkers who come this way will get wet feet. Walkers who wish to avoid the ford are recommended to follow the main path which descends to the Rawthey by a footbridge (698970) near the Cross Keys Inn, walk along the A683 for the best part of a mile to Handley's Bridge (706976) shortly after a lay-by, then ascend the access lane to Narthwaite farm. For ford users, the NC route leaves the main path shortly before its descent to the 698970 footbridge. It climbs gradually then contours along the Backside valley until it reaches the ford. After crossing the beck the way is up a stony track to Narthwaite.

Just west of the farmyard at Narthwaite turn north up a stony track which climbs beside a wall on the right. Soon bear right at a fork (702976), still beside the wall, but this soon ends. The track from Narthwaite to Adamthwaite is nearly two miles long and was once a route of some importance, passing three residences whose ruins remain by the wayside. Today in places the path is a fine green lane, but more often it has become boggy. The way is well trodden and provides fine views eastward, especially to Wild Boar Fell and Harter Fell. Eventually there is a choice of routes: take the right fork, between walls. Remote Adamthwaite farm (710999) containing a spinning gallery is passed soon afterwards. Go through the farm and take the metalled access road. This is a lonely unfenced moorland lane which climbs for half a mile to cross a flank of the Howgills. It continues, generally downhill, for two miles to Ravenstonedale. At Town Head, the main route is joined.

STAGE 4: RAVENSTONEDALE to APPLEBY

Distance 14.9miles/24kms
Ascent 970ft/300m

1:25,000 Maps
Outdoor Leisure 19 - Howgill Fells

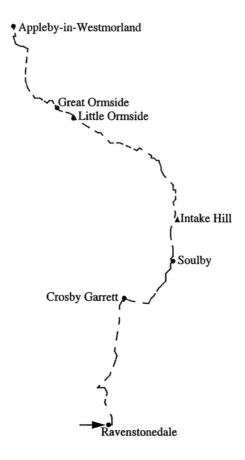

After two days in the hills, today's walk is an interlude in the plain before another upland session. Throughout the day you are within a mile of the River Eden or its tributary Scandal Beck but there is sufficient variety so that it does not seem like a valley walk. Only rarely is the route beside the river.

Leave Ravenstonedale by turning right by the Black Swan on a lane that crosses Scandal Beck. Soon turn left on a byway which becomes a grassy track between walls. It leads to the old A685; almost opposite at 724043 take a footpath which bridges a stream in the field. Exit the field via a step stile in a wall, some distance left of the gate. Beyond the wall are steps down to the new A685 bypass. Cross carefully and rejoin the path which initially is accompanied by a cart track. The path continues north, left of a copse, and then bears left round a rise. Soon Smardale Bridge is seen ahead. Aim for this, keeping parallel to but above Scandal Beck on the left. Join an ancient highway and turn left over Smardale Bridge. Then fork right and upward on the path used by Wainwright's Coast to Coast route, crossing over a disused railway (722062). (In recent years members of the public have been permitted to walk along this railway trackbed which crosses the Scandal Beck by the majestic Smardalegill Viaduct. An alternative to the NC route from Smardale Bridge to Smardale Mill (3 miles) follows the railway to near Smardale Hall (739082) then takes Beck Lane and the riverside path.) After climbing to a step stile in a nearby wall the NC leaves Wainwright's route and enters a long field, following Scandal Beck, and with a wall not far away on the right. After the long field there is a succession of smaller fields over the next mile and eventually the path joins a clear bridleway at the side of open fells. This continues under the viaduct of the Settle & Carlisle railway into Crosby Garrett village.

It is tempting to spend some time looking round Crosby Garrett, a picturesque farming village with a prominent parish church on a hill. Lanes run on both sides of the village stream and there are many linking bridges. It is here that today's walk changes character. Until Crosby Garrett you have been in open fell country, with uncultivated fields, few visible dwellings, and fine views of hills nearby. The rest of the day is spent in farmland, amongst pleasant surroundings, but they lack the untamed grandeur of the fells.

Follow the lane on the right of the village stream, past Crosby Garrett United Church. Just beyond the former Mossgill Chapel (729095) turn right on a path between walls. It soon becomes a broad green track and descends into a pasture field. Keep straight on in the centre of this field, but in the next field veer left and cross the fence by a gate into a rough lane (733093). This soon enters another field: follow the right hand fence over a rise and pass through a gate into an overgrown old lane (736092). Turn left along this lane, down to meet Scandal Beck near Smardale Mill. This time do not cross it. Instead go over a stile on the left and through a gate on the right into a lush green pasture. Continue close to the river through green fields accompanied by trees for nearly a mile, crossing Far Leases Lane which fords the beck. At Soulby Mill the path joins a metalled lane which is taken to a road. Turn right to a crossroads in the centre of Soulby. This is another pleasant village which has a large green beside the river.

Leave Soulby on the road going north. When it is clear of the village it makes a sharp left turn; at this point (749115) continue straight on along a farm lane to Sykeside. Beyond the farm, after the first metal gate bear diagonally left for the next gate in the field corner. Continue ahead, rising over the side of Intake Hill passing left of a metal barn. Bear left and descend to meet a lane by a metal gate (750129). Cross over, take the footbridge just to the right, and continue ahead through three fields to a stile with a small footbridge over a ditch. Bear right, contouring around Cowber Hill to join the concrete access track to Ploughlands (750138). Just before the farm, look out on the left for a waymarked path which takes walkers round the farm and up a field to join an old lane that is another access to Ploughlands. Continue along this lane. The River Eden comes into view and the path descends beside the river to Warcop Old Bridge. This is a pleasant spot, often visited by motorists for relaxing by (and in) the river.

Much of the route between Warcop Bridge and Little Ormside is on clear tracks and bridleways. At the bridge stay west of the Eden and briefly join the road, but soon leave it for a lane beside the river. At 740153 turn left along a rising bridleway north westward. Ignore a clear track going left at 737154. At 734155, ignore the obvious track off left downhill and follow the right hand boundary through a gate. Thereafter follow field boundaries on a ridge and then descend to Sandford Bridge but again do not cross the Eden. Turn left through Blacksyke farmyard, then take a waymarked gate on the right into a wood. The path climbs and eventually emerges into a field. It continues as a farm track and then as a lane into Little Ormside. Bear right, and soon cross over Helm Beck. Just after the bridge turn left (707169) along a path across a few fields to meet a lane. Turn right on this into Great Ormside.

In the centre of Great Ormside village there is a triangle of roads. At this point (701173) take a signed footpath on the west between gardens and across a field to meet a lane. Turn left and pass under the railway bridge. The path then bears left but at 697173 it turns sharp right, crossing Jeremy Gill by a footbridge (695175). It rises to follow the edge of a wood for some 600yds, then descends steeply in the wood to water level, and continues beside the Eden, a bit too close for comfort at times. Eventually the wood ends and the path continues as a pleasant riverside walk. As Appleby is approached the footpath leaves the Eden and crosses Castle Bank on an enclosed path to reach a lane. Turn left up to the B6260, and follow this into the centre of the town.

STAGE 5: APPLEBY to LANGDON BECK

Distance 16.6miles/26.7kms
Ascent 2230ft/780m

1:25,000 Maps
Outdoor Leisure 19 - Howgill Fells
Outdoor Leisure 31 - N Pennines, Teesdale & Weardale

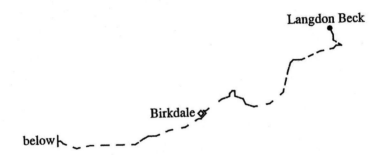

Langdon Beck

Birkdale

below

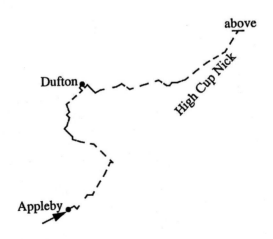

above

Dufton

High Cup Nick

Appleby

Appleby is a town well worth visiting. Many walkers will want to stay here for a few hours and then travel four miles through fields and woods to an overnight stop in Dufton, continuing to Langdon Beck on the following day. Ramblers who consider themselves tough, and those with limited time, will no doubt prefer to tackle the full distance in one go. This is the day when the main Pennine ridge is crossed and it is one of the highlights of the Northern Crossway. Dramatic sights such as High Cup Gill and Cauldron Snout will long remain in the memory. This route is also used by the Pennine Way; curiously, northbound followers of the Northern Crossway and the Pennine Way use this track in opposite directions.

From the Market Place in the centre of Appleby pass over the River Eden and cross the main road (the old A66) by a zebra crossing. Continue along an ascending tarmac footpath beside Sands Methodist Church, then bearing left to reach Garth Heads Road. Ascend Clifford Street nearly opposite, almost reaching the railway station, but turn left at the Midland Hotel and then right under the railway. (Alternatively pass through the station and use its footbridge. Appleby station is on the Settle-Carlisle line and is most attractively presented with flower baskets and 'Victorian' platform lamps.)

Take the road upward passing Appleby Primary School and the level crossing of a railway not currently in use. Where the road turns right, continue ahead on a footpath which crosses the busy A66 followed by a lane and take the stile opposite. Cross a field bearing slightly right to reach a minor lane (689210). Go left but when the lane turns right keep straight on over a stile (689212). After a few fields the path becomes a green lane between hedges. It then passes through the garden of Clickham Cottage to reach a road junction. Keep straight on along a road which has wide verges at first. After a quarter mile turn right along a footpath through Croft Ends Farm (678228) into a long field. Keep in the centre of this field to a stile in a stone wall and then through a gate to a road. Turn left for a few paces. (Ahead is Brampton, a biggish village with accommodation, an inn, but no shop.) Use a stile into a field on the right and descend to a stile in the bottom hedge. Immediately go over a footbridge on the right, then another on the left, and turn left to meet a rough lane. Turn right on this, and in a short distance where it forks (682236), turn right uphill into an attractive green lane called Wood Lane. After about a mile this becomes a footpath and drops through Dufton Ghyll Wood, crosses the stream by a footbridge and then climbs to emerge onto Dufton village green. As well as being a delightful village, Dufton boasts a cafe/shop, an inn, a youth hostel and other places of accommodation.

Dufton marks the boundary between the plain and the hills. Much of the spectacular route ahead can boast an obvious path, but it is less clear in the marshy ground above 1750ft so care is needed especially in mist.

Take the road eastward through Dufton village centre, and as it descends beyond the village, turn left along a lane signposted to 'High Cup Nick' (694248). This has a long steady climb, and its condition gradually deteriorates into a footpath. At a point where a walker's gate is near a stile (722250), the track fragments into several paths. Go straight ahead on a rising path through a gully past a cairn, and continue on a good track marked by a series of cairns. It runs parallel to High Cup Gill, a deep valley with very steep sides, and walkers should not stray too close to the edge. The valley ends abruptly at High Cupgill Head (746262) and it is worth pausing to experience the remarkable sight of the full valley, resembling an enormous hole dug out of the hillside by an immense excavator, and yet possessing such an incongruously small river for its size.

Continue north east and soon reach the highest point of the day's walk (about 1920ft). It is the Pennine watershed; behind you the streams flow into the Eden and those ahead join the Tees. Keep north east for over a mile along a well trodden green track which descends gradually and crosses the Maize Beck by a footbridge at 766268. It continues beside the river for a while, then rises through the moors, keeping left of military 'Keep Out' signs. A footbridge over Grain Beck marks the end of the moorland. Ahead, the path reaches green fields and the lonely farm buildings of Birkdale (804278). It uses Birkdale's access lane for a mile until it crosses the River Tees. On the left is the dam of Cow Green Reservoir, but your route turns right, a scramble down the rocks where hands as well as feet are needed! Beside the rocks is the spectacular series of waterfalls called Cauldron Snout: when in spate this becomes a sea of gushing foam. (Walkers who prefer not to do the scramble can take the road to Langdon Beck instead.)

There is a complete change of scenery at the foot of Cauldron Snout. Instead of wild open moorland, you are now in a long deep craggy valley containing the wide flood plain of the River Tees and with little room for anything else, even the footpath. The Tees is soon joined by Maize Beck, now swollen with the contents of many mountain streams. The path runs close to the river for nearly two miles, including some places where more rock scrambling is necessary. Then green fields are the scene for another mile as the riverside path continues in more placid surroundings, past Widdy Bank Farm nearby. Eventually the path leaves the Tees (844299) and passes through fields for a good half mile to meet its tributary the Harwood Beck, at Saur Hill Bridge (855302). Do not cross the bridge (unless aiming for Langdon Beck Youth Hostel). Turn left on a path parallel to Harwood Beck, eventually descending to the river side and then through Intake Farm. Cross the river by a low concrete fording bridge to meet a minor road (852309). (To reach the Langdon Beck Hotel turn right and follow the road up to the B6277.)

STAGE 6: LANGDON BECK to COWSHILL

Distance 8.9miles/14.3kms
Ascent 1320ft/406m

1:25,000 Maps
Outdoor Leisure 31 - N Pennines, Teesdale & Weardale

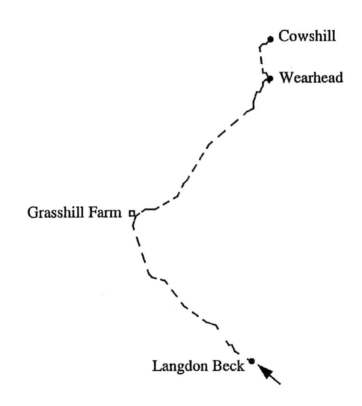

It is a short walk today, first through peaceful Harwood Dale with its picturesque scattered white farms and cottages. Then the Grasshill Causeway is followed over the moors and down into Weardale. Hardy walkers may wish to continue to Rookhope and then on to Hexham the next day, but most ramblers will prefer not to have such high mileages each day when out in the hills. Today's walk is not necessarily as simple as it sounds; all day is spent above 1100ft and the route exceeds 2200ft at its highest point.

The road from Langdon Beck to Cow Green crosses Harwood Beck at 850309. Leave the road here and follow a signed footpath along the north side of the beck. After a ladder stile this leaves the riverside and climbs diagonally right to meet the B6277 at 842319. From this point the B6277 was rerouted in turnpike days. We follow the old formation of the road, which begins as a tarmac lane to Green Hills farm. Beyond the farm it continues as a grassy path across several fields but it has become a cart track by the time it reaches Lingy Hill farm.

The way ahead is metalled and it meets the road serving Harwood valley. Follow this road to its lowest point, where it crosses two streams. On the left a farm track leaves for Stoney Hill: just after this turn right along a bridleway (820334). This was once an access track to Grass Hill Farm, which at nearly 2000 feet was the highest farm in the country until it was abandoned in 1942. The bridleway is a clearly visible track which climbs steadily to cross the B6277 at 816345, passing out of pasture fields into moorland. North of the B-road the route passes through a gate and continues as a path visible on the ground, at first close to the road. Pass Hawk Sike Hush (815349) and climb up the field keeping close to the wall on the left, then meet a stony lane at 816353 near the neat ruins of Grass Hill Farm.

The stony lane is the Grasshill Causeway. It ascends from Harwood Dale to a summit at Coldberry End (2200ft) and then has a long descent into Weardale. From the causeway there are fine views of both valleys and the surrounding hills, including the Cross Fell range. From Coldberry End it is a short climb to the trig point on High Field (2322ft) which is another fine viewpoint.

Grasshill Causeway is followed for over three miles. As it descends to Weardale its surface gradually improves and it becomes a normally metalled lane by the time it meets the road from Burnhope Reservoir dam. Then farms appear, not all occupied. After passing access lanes on the left to High Rigg and Middle Rigg, at 855387 take an unsigned track left to a nearby farm. Where the track swings right into the farmyard, keep straight on through a gate, with a wall on the left. Keep beside the wall as it bears right and continue between walls. Pass right of Low Rigg, currently decayed, and descend to meet the road from Wear Valley water treatment works. Turn right to the A689 at Wearhead.

It is at Wearhead that Killhope and Burnhope Burns meet to create the River Wear. The village is on the Cowshill-Stanhope bus route and has a shop. Turn left along the A689 (Front St) over the newly formed River Wear and go past the Village Hall. Take a left lane towards a school, but after crossing the Killhope Burn (857397) turn right along a grassy riverside footpath through fields. Near an abandoned house on the left, the path climbs a bank and runs beside a wall. Round the corner it reaches a road (854405); turn right over the burn, then right again along a rough lane. When this lane bears right over a stream, keep straight on in front of some cottages, and climb steps beyond. Soon the path reaches the A689 by the Cowshill Hotel. But be careful! The A689 is crossed at a sharp bend and there is no pavement. So beware of passing motor traffic.

STAGE 7: COWSHILL to BLANCHLAND

Distance 12.7miles/20.5kms
Ascent 2000ft/615m

1:25,000 Maps
Outdoor Leisure 31 - N Pennines, Teesdale & Weardale
Explorer 307 - Consett & Derwent Reservoir

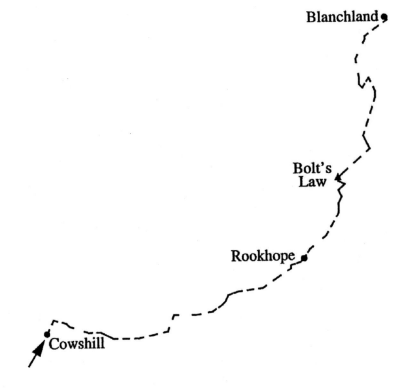

This is a day spent almost entirely in open moorland. The area has been a prolific lead mining region and you will see many signs of old workings. The route follows some of their transport routes by packhorse and by rail.

Immediately after reaching the A689 turn right over a stream and then go sharp left on a rough road. It follows the stream and ascends gradually, initially passing through industrial premises. Just before a house on the left the lane forks. Take the right fork, then opposite the house turn right through a north-facing gate (860411) and climb steadily amidst old spoil heaps. This is a former packhorse track used for carrying lead to Newcastle and other places. Named Sedling Rake, it becomes a broad track beside a wall, commanding fine views over Weardale: Burnhope Reservoir and yesterday's route along Grasshill Causeway are clearly seen.

It is a pity to reach the end of this pleasant track. Beyond a short wood a lane is joined (885405). The NC continues to follow the packhorse route for 2.5 miles, but this part of the route is metalled. However, it is a lonely lane with wide verges and few cars. Turn left, descend Middlehope Bank, cross the burn and then climb to Scarsike Head (911413) on the ridge overlooking the Rookhope Burn valley. Keep on the lane which descends towards Lintzgarth Plantation. But as it curves left to reach the trees, leave it by taking a ladder stile on the right (918419).

Two paths leave the road at this point. Take the left hand one, signed "Lead Mining Trail", which soon passes through a gate. (Alternatively, another ladder stile by Lintzgarth Plantation can be used: this route has slightly more road and less swamp than the right of way.) At first this is featureless bogland with occasional paths and waymarks. Aim for Boltslaw Incline, seen across the valley. Eventually you reach a pool. Keep left of this and use two stiles over wire fences. A clear path continues, soon joined by a fence, and when it forks go right via a minor spoil heap and then left of a modern metal shed. Turn left onto this shed's access track and go over a ladder stile on to a rough lane. Turn right on this past Prydale House, then veer left downhill. By Broad Dale House take a path on the right down the slope to a stile. Here on the right are remnants of industrial buildings. Go ahead along a rough road over Rookhope Burn to the road in the centre of the village. The Rookhope Inn is on the right and the village shop is round the corner. Rookhope's war memorial is unusual in that as well as naming its 1914-1918 dead, it names those who returned.

Leave the village centre on a rough stony ascending track "leading to Hylton Terrace". The Sustrans Coast-to-Coast cycle route also takes this. Keep to the main upward way, then fork left onto the formation of the Boltslaw railway incline of the Weardale Iron Company. It was built in 1846 and was about 2000 yards long, with a gradient of 1 in 12. Ironstone, lead and other produce of the Rookhope area travelled up the incline and over the moors beyond to join the remarkable Stanhope & Tyne railway of 1834: this went over the hills via several more inclines to reach the river at

South Shields. It is a long and steady climb up from Rookhope village and it is worth stopping part way up to admire the views westward. At the top of the incline the route enters a cutting and ruins can be seen of the stone locomotive shed. Formerly there were other structures in this remote spot, including a winding engine with a large chimney and a row of cottages. At 1670ft this was the highest-ever point of the standard-gauge railway system in the whole of the British Isles. The line closed in 1923, but on the relatively level section above the incline rails remained in position until 1943. Some sleeper marks remain.

Ahead there is a change of scenery onto heather slopes which are reminiscent of the North Yorkshire Moors. The NC continues along the railway trackbed for half a mile beyond the incline. By a sheepfold on the right (953450), take a faint footpath on the left, and cross a wire fence by a stile marked by a tall post. Turn left, following the general line of the fence, to the summit of Bolt's Law, 1773ft. If visibility is good, there are fine views in all directions. Notice Sikehead Reservoir, a short mile away on the north-east, with long-disused chimneys each side of it. The NC will pass the right-hand one.

Retrace your steps from Bolt's Law summit for a short distance to a gate and then descend on a clear path aiming north-east. At a footpath crossing continue straight ahead past an isolated tree to a gate. Do not go through the gate but turn left on a narrow path which crosses a stream three times on flags. Turn right off this to reach the chimney beside the reservoir, one of the few landmarks in the moorland. Walk north beside the reservoir, then turn right through a gate on a good stony track. Soon this crosses another track: turn left here but later when the major way bears right, keep straight on. A small wood on the hillside ahead is a good guide. The unfenced Blanchland to Stanhope road is reached at 963479.

Go left for half a mile then left again at a road junction (959485). Soon, just after the road bends right, take a broad descending footpath through a gate on the right for a short distance, then fork right along a level path. At first this path has a wall on the right for company, but later enters Deborah Plantation and eventually joins a forest track back to the road (958497). Turn left downhill, then almost opposite a lane on the left turn right on a path through woodland, parallel to the River Derwent. It comes out on the B6306: turn left over the Derwent and into the centre of Blanchland, one of the most picturesque villages in the whole of England. It would be nice to spend time here and patronise the village shops and cafes. But if you haven't booked accommodation in advance, you need to be aware that supply is limited here, and the bus service is sparse.

STAGE 8: BLANCHLAND to HEXHAM

Distance 13.8miles/22.1kms
Ascent 1500ft/462m

1:25,000 Maps
Outdoor Leisure 43 - Hadrian's Wall

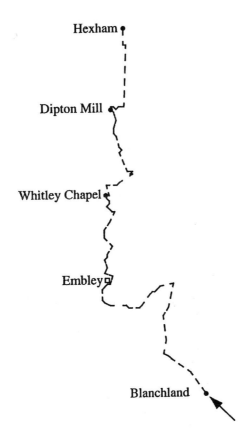

Today's route starts in open heather moorland, then follows (not too closely) the valley of the river known as Devil's Water, and then takes to pasture fields as it approaches the River Tyne and Hexham.

From Blanchland village centre take the lane ahead on the left of the former village school (now a tearoom). It climbs steadily past Shildon (960511) where a ruined engine house on the left is a reminder of former lead mines. The lane continues to a final cottage, curiously named Pennypie House, once an inn on an important drove road. Beyond is moorland: go through the gate and bear right on a stony track beside a wall. It curves right, still climbing, and then passes through a gate into open heather moors for 1.5 miles. Views include Derwent Reservoir and Bolt's Law.

Slaley Forest is ahead. Shortly before reaching it, at 953545 turn left on a faint path, a green way amongst the heather. It soon enters woodland by a ladder stile and meets a forestry road. Turn left and follow it westward, ignoring two tracks on the right. At the plantation boundary (944541) two bridleways continue ahead: take the right hand one through the heather of Embley Fell. As it descends towards the valley of Devil's Water it is joined by a byway, and becomes wider and more stony. The bridleway gets close to the river at Embley Bank, but then it forks right and climbs through four fields to reach Embley farm.

Continue on Embley's stony access lane for over a mile. After crossing a stream by a ford it becomes properly metalled. Soon afterwards bear right uphill on a lane at a fork (928556). A quarter-mile after this take a path left using a stile almost hidden in a gorse bush. The path descends steeply in a thistle field: aim slightly to the right to find a walker's gate in the far corner (928561). Close to the river the path joins a sunken lane: follow this old lane as it crosses both Devil's Water and the Raw Burn by fords, in each case accompanied by a footbridge. After the second bridge follow the sign to Low Rawgreen, taking a climbing path through a wood into a field. Low Rawgreen farm is ahead: go to a stile just left of it, then walk across the front of its buildings and climb a ladder stile into a rough field.

On this new path keep close to the right hand side of two fields, then take a ladder stile on the right into a wood. Here there is a clear level path which runs close to Devil's Water again. When the path forks, keep right to stay close to the river. But when the path reaches a footbridge over the river (931572) turn left on an ascending path. Soon fork right through a gully and exit the wood into a field with Moss House ahead. Pass just left of the building, and join the farm's entrance track which climbs to a road. Turn right to the cross roads in the centre of Whitley Chapel village with distinctive clean yellow stone buildings.

Take the eastbound road out of Whitley Chapel as far as 929577, and here take a signed path on the left. As you approach Mollersteads take the gate on the right as this is the start of the next path to be taken. It follows field boundaries, initially on the right and then on the left. At the entrance to a wood, pass over a stile and a nearby walker's gate and continue on the outside of the wood until the next stile is reached at 933583. Here enter the wood and descend to Rowley Burn and follow this as far as a road near Dye House. Turn left over the burn and then go immediately right on a footpath still beside the river, then cross a field to a stile left of some houses. Turn left on the ensuing track which turns and climbs steeply up to rejoin the road at Juniper (938587).

Turn sharp left along the road, but after a few yards take a tarmac drive on the right. This drive too is soon forsaken: turn right on a path which climbs gently beside a wall, then passes through a brief wood and three further fields to reach a road at Smelting Syke (934595). Turn left, then soon go right over a ladder stile onto a path signed 'Dotland Park'. Go diagonally left across a large field to a gate in the far corner, and join a track which curves right to reach Dotland Park farm. Turn left along the farm's metalled access road. Where this meets Hill Road, go straight across, following a hedged stony lane which descends to a major road at Diptonmill Inn (929610).

Cross the river at Diptonmill, then turn right on a clear path, signed 'Hole House'. This follows the burn as far as a path junction near a footbridge; here turn left for Hole House. The path passes to the right of the house, then climbs through a wood and several fields onto a road (935624) from which you receive your first views of Hexham and the Tyne valley. The path continues in the same direction but now downhill, until it emerges onto a road. Turn right, downhill, but immediately after Elvaston Drive joins on the left, go through a hole in the left wall (936633). This is the entrance to a long walled passage called Long Nick. Where it comes out onto Gaprigg Lane turn left and then take the first road right, St Wilfrid's Road, to reach the busy main road (the old A69) in the centre of Hexham. Cross this and take Beaumont Road opposite to reach Hexham Market Place, beside the Abbey.

Hexham is the largest town on the Northern Crossway. It is just over the halfway point for northbound walkers, and contains several historic buildings well worth visiting, so it makes an ideal place for a rest day. Even if you are unable to stop for long, you will probably need to obtain provisions, as there are few shops between here and Wooler, five nights away.

STAGE 9: HEXHAM to WARK

Distance 13.5miles/21.6kms
Ascent 1420ft/437m

1:25,000 Maps
Outdoor Leisure 43 - Hadrian's Wall

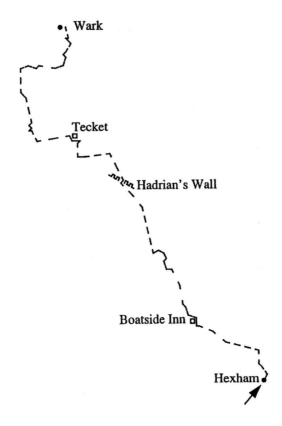

Wark

Tecket

Hadrian's Wall

Boatside Inn

Hexham

The River Tyne has two principal tributaries, appropriately called the North Tyne and the South Tyne. Both pass through picturesque scenery before they join 1.5 miles west of Hexham. The journey today begins with a mile beside the combined river, soon crosses over the South Tyne then continues in modest hills before returning to the North Tyne at Wark.

At Hexham Market Place cross over to the front right hand corner of the Abbey and take the paved path which runs along its right hand side. It goes under an archway then passes a bowling green on the right and a children's play area on the left. Beyond a school take a path between railings that slopes down and curves, bridging over the Cockshaw Burn to meet a minor road. Turn right along this road beside the stream: it bears left, still beside the stream, and leads to a multiple road junction where the stream is culverted. Curve left and cross the major road onto a road with the stream re-emerging on its right. This road is called Tyne Green Road, and if it lacks a nameplate it can be identified by the TVR garage "Hexham Horseless Carriages" on the left at the start, and by a bus garage on the left later on.

At the end of Tyne Green Road continue ahead to a level crossing with the Newcastle-Carlisle railway, heralded by a crossing keeper's florid cottage. Keep straight on across the golf course, following an indistinct bridleway. On reaching the River Tyne (933650) turn left along an excellent path beside the wide river. Too many trees hinder views across but the river can be heard even if not seen. Beyond the golf course the railway comes close on the left and indeed the path occupies a tiny space between railway and river. Until 1956 the Border Counties Railway left the main line here and crossed the river en route for the North Tyne valley: bridge foundations can still be seen in the river, - if the trees reveal gaps.

The path gains a tarmac surface, leaves the riverside, passes under the A69 bypass, then becomes a lane continuing past West Boat to meet a road at 910659. Turn right over the river, which is now the South Tyne. The bridge dates from 1903 and is guarded by a cottage where tolls were collected. The previous means of crossing the river is marked by the Boatside Inn of 1837 and a riverside cottage.

Take the road ahead (to the right of the Boatside Inn), then immediately after passing under the railway, turn left on a footpath. This runs beside the railway to some houses named Quality Cottages. Here turn right climbing on a good track. The path eventually levels out and provides good views of Fourstones village and the South Tyne valley. It continues as a pleasant track in a wood, then gently descends to the left of an isolated cottage, whose long access track is then followed north to the B6319 at Whinny Hill (896686). Here turn left by a power station, then turn right on a road for a mile, generally uphill. When it has levelled off at 890704 leave it by a ladder stile in the wall on the left, signed 'Military Road'. Head diagonally right across a field corner then continue across a big field aiming for the left end of a row of tall trees. When you reach this an empty building comes into view. Pass through a copse left of the building, into a large field. Aim slightly right downhill to reach a stile. The path continues uphill to a gate onto the B6318, the busy military road (883713). It is a good viewpoint: on a clear day you can see back to Bolts Law and the Cross Fell range. Shortly, looking forward, Chipchase Castle, the North Tyne Valley and the Cheviots become visible.

Cross the B6318 and take the lane opposite. In a few yards cross Hadrian's Wall. Continue along the lane for a short mile to Sharpley (878723) and turn left on a bridleway which passes through a field and rises to a gate in the far left corner, then continues beside a wall, parallel to Hadrian's Wall which can be observed about three fields away. You can appreciate the strategic importance of locating the Wall in this lonely upland and windswept area: long distance views make it an ideal defensive position. Opposite a gate on the left, take the track descending right to a gateway. The track turns north and then curves east towards Uppertown farm. But before the farm buildings are reached, turn sharp left and very soon right through a wicket gate. The path drops into a wooded ravine and crosses a river. The ensuing climb can be eased by following the stream to a telegraph pole and then zigzagging up the slope to a stile west of Tecket farm. Cross a small field to a lane (864730).

Turn left on this for a mile until the tarmac ends just after passing a fortified house on the left (851728). Here turn right, for a few yards on the entrance track to Stoup Rigg Farm: where this goes off left, continue straight ahead on a moorland track for over a mile. This is the wildest part of this stage: fields and farms are replaced by untamed grasses and wetland. Three broad streams are crossed: there is a bridge over the first but the others do not have this luxury. Sometimes the track curves to ease the gradient and it is easy to lose direction: be careful to keep close to the wall, or the mound which succeeds it. Further north aim for Pit Wood and go round its left side to meet the access lane to Goatstones farm. Turn right on this and continue to Ward Lane (845751).

Go straight across onto a farm lane. After a gate across it, take a good track on the right which gradually falls to meet another near Bleaklaw (a barn) (848756). Continue eastward through Conshield farmyard and use the gate on the left (not the one straight ahead) to reach a path that follows field boundaries through an abundance of nettles to Latterford Doors (863759). Turn left along the access lane to a ford with adjoining footbridge, and take a short right path beside the river to return to the lane at Latterford. Continue to the B6320 and turn left. After crossing Warks Burn, turn right on a footpath beside the River North Tyne to Wark Bridge built in 1878. Turn left for Wark, an interesting village, which has a shop, inns, a market square and a town hall-cum-mechanics institute.

STAGE 10: WARK to ELSDON

Distance 14.3miles/22.9kms
Ascent 1760ft/542m

1:25,000 Maps
Outdoor Leisure 43 - Hadrian's Wall
Outdoor Leisure 42 - Kielder Water

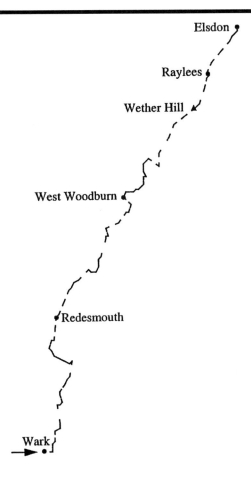

Elsdon

Raylees

Wether Hill

West Woodburn

Redesmouth

Wark

The walk today is in two distinct parts, separated by West Woodburn. The first part is in an upland area with sparse vegetation, more suitable for sheep than cows, yet never far from rivers North Tyne and Rede. There is a sense of history around, as the route meets a disused railway and an ancient highway, then passes the site of a Roman fort. Beyond West Woodburn is the ascent of Wether Hill, through afforested moorland. Throughout the day there are fine views.

Cross over Wark Bridge and turn left at the T-junction. The lane soon leaves the riverside. At a fork turn left and carry on for about a mile upward with good views across the valley. After passing Thornyhirst, an isolated cottage, turn right at 864788 but soon leave the lane as it curves left by taking a walkers' gate on the left into a field. Aim to the right of a historic building named as `Bastle' on the Ordnance Survey map. Use a ladder stile just beyond the building, then turn right and continue ahead beside a wall/fence on the right. Where this ends, go down a short steep slope and through a gate on the left. Continue left of straight ahead to a narrow gate in a left side fence. From here (hidden) stone steps lead down to the trackbed of an abandoned railway (869798).

This was the Border Counties Railway which the NC crossed at Hexham. Do not continue on the path to the North Tyne, shown on the map, as it can be dangerous. Instead turn right along the railway formation through a cutting for about half a mile, then take the first gate on the right to a lane at Heugh, 872805. This is a quiet location today, but it was busy in 1860: for fourteen months the railway terminated here, and ongoing passengers had to continue their journeys along the narrow lanes. Follow the lane left under the former railway and over Heugh Burn, then go left along a footpath in front of a house (869804). This is a pleasant woodland path which gets close to the North Tyne and follows it through Countesspark Wood. In the heart of the wood you pass an unusual wooden cabin with an enormous brick chimney.

Eventually the path leaves the river and the wood behind and climbs towards the old railway. Fork right up steps and over a ladder stile to rejoin the trackbed. Turn left and soon reach a station at a junction. Throughout its life it was called Reedsmouth Junction, but the correct spelling of the adjacent village is Redesmouth. On the left the line continued to Bellingham, Kielder, and on into Scotland; the line on the right went via Scotsgap to Morpeth. The signal box at the junction has been converted to a private residence, and so has the platform building on the right. Other railway structures have survived, including a small engine shed beside the Bellingham line, now used as a farm store. The path takes the left fork, and beyond the platform it turns right through a field to a junction of lanes. Bear right to the road, and take the path opposite signed to 'Rede Bridge'.

North of Redesmouth a mile of railway trackbed has become a public footpath, and the NC quickly rejoins the railway formation. Near Rede Bridge there was a level crossing whose keeper's cottage remains by the lineside. The lane here was an important mediaeval highway: Rede Bridge (5 minutes walk away on the left) is substantial, one of only two river crossings between Wark and West Woodburn, but now unused by vehicles. On the NC continue straight ahead towards a bridge over the trackbed (872835); just before it, follow the waymark off left, onto an old track at first beside the railway then veering left away from it, and visible as a lush green way passing through a field of scrub. It crosses Broomhope Burn by a footbridge (877839) and then rises to meet a tarmac lane.

Turn right on the lane which passes under the railway route, and then rises. It turns right at a cattle grid (883841): leave it here for a footpath. It is shown on the map as going diagonally left to reach a gate into the wood. However it goes through marshy land, so it is easier to follow the wall (not too close) and then the edge of the wood to reach the gate. Once in the wood, the path is awkward to find as it is waymarked only intermittently and some farm tracks look more important. Pass to the right of Calf Close, an isolated cottage, and keep to a generally northerly direction. Beyond some pens for birds, go right at a T-junction to reach a walkers' gate at the edge of the wood. Do not pass through it but turn left along the woodland edge, following the wall on your right, until a waymarked stile on the right is reached, hiding behind bracken. Pass over this stile into a field and continue on a northward path along the right wall boundary. After two fields and a bridge over the former railway, castellated Cragg Farm lies ahead (886854).

The path passes to the right of Cragg Farm, then heads diagonally right uphill. In the next fields follow the right hand boundary to reach a good viewpoint where the earthworks of the Roman fort Habitancum can be seen clearly, with West Woodburn village beyond. Descend to a gate just left of the field's bottom right hand corner. At this point the route of the Roman road Dere Street, which served Habitancum, is crossed; although there is no obvious sign of the road here, in the left distance a wall follows its course climbing the hillside. The NC veers left to a bridge over a stream, then continues upward passing right of Broadgate. At the top of the climb turn left and enter a field: follow a path diagonally to emerge via a squeeze stile onto the fast A68 main road at West Woodburn. Be careful as there is no pavement at this point. Turn left.

West Woodburn village offers accommodation, an inn, a tea room, and a village shop/post office. Follow the A68 across the River Rede and past the Bay Horse Inn, then take the next minor road on the right. Turn right beside the river, then after passing a lane on the left followed by Peel Cottage, take a left path diagonally through a field to a step stile in the wall. Keep in the same direction to East Woodburn Bridge over the Rede (901876). This bridge is unexpectedly substantial for a route used mainly by walkers, indicating that the track must once have been an important highway, probably in the days before Woodburn got its own church, as the whole area was served by the isolated church at Corsenside (890893). After crossing the bridge, turn left and soon pass over a stream by a footbridge. Go left briefly then fork right uphill on a clear path. When almost at a fence, the path curves left and crosses the fence later at a stile. It continues to a lane at 902883 beside the access drive from Yearhaugh Farm. Turn right along the lane for a short distance.

The highlight of this stage's walk is the climb over Wether Hill. At 906880 take a path on the left signed 'Raylees 2.5 miles'. Immediately the forest is entered, on a waymarked track, at first rather narrow, progressing steadily uphill. The route has several little planks helpfully placed across streams. It passes a Vodafone transmitter and continues along a wider track. It crosses two walls. After the second one (909890), the way is not obvious: go right, then soon left following a firebreak, at first downhill. Eventually the path comes out of the wood but then fragments. The official right of way follows the forest boundary, but this is rough walking, and it is easier to take a track west of this which eventually returns to the boundary. Pass through a gate by the wood end to reach the trig point on Wether Hill summit just beyond (920903).

This is a good viewpoint: Raylees in the valley ahead looks temptingly close. It is marked by a clump of trees behind on the left. Aim for a wall on the right and cross this by a ladder stile. Then head straight towards the house below. When you reach it pass left of the buildings, cross Raylees Burn by a footbridge, then go up to the A696. From here a minor road opposite leads directly to the attractive village of Elsdon with its wide village green. It has an inn, a cafe and some accommodation.

STAGE 11: ELSDON to ALWINTON

Distance 15.3miles/24.5kms
Ascent 1660ft/511m

1:25,000 Maps
Outdoor Leisure 42 - Kielder Water
Outdoor Leisure 16 - Cheviot Hills

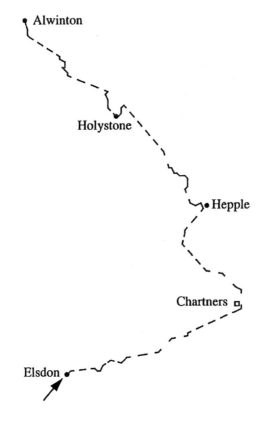

The walk today like yesterday is in two parts. But today the afforested moorland of Harwood Forest comes first, and its lack of a proper path makes passage through it an ordeal not a pleasure. The peaceful Coquet valley comes as welcome relief afterwards and there are wonderful views of the Cheviots ahead.

From Elsdon go briefly north on the B6341 to cross the brook. Then turn right on the unfenced lane to Landshot. Beyond all the buildings of Landshot Farm turn left at 948934 on a waymarked path and go over a ladder stile. Cross a stream by a visible footbridge and continue uphill, following the right hand wall. In the top corner (954938), not far from the summit of Landshot Hill, turn right and follow another wall; if the path is lost in bracken go higher up. Cross a ladder stile on the right and continue beside the wall into Harwood Forest at 959936.

The path shown on the map, going north-east through Harwood Forest, is largely non-existent so you have a choice: either follow the perimeter of the forest outside it, or use firebreaks within the woodland. In both cases the ground is rough, there is no obvious path on the ground, and there are awkward streams and marshy areas to cross. It is easy to get disoriented in woodland, and if you are uncertain about your compass navigational skills, you may prefer to take the exterior route, north east via King's Dod, Dough Crag and Darden Rigg to meet a bridleway at 994970.

For those who accept the challenge of the forest, at the entrance bear left along the visible firebreak. At a clearing veer left beside heather then rejoin the firebreak by turning right at the end of the clearing (966940). The firebreak veers left and reaches a second clearing (971942). Cut across the rough ground here and re-enter the firebreak. Then at a third clearing (976945) the forest boundary can be seen nearby on the left. Keep to the right in crossing this clearing to benefit from a hidden bridge over a stream. The occasional waymark also makes an appearance. Shortly after this clearing, pass a sheepfold on the left and continue down the firebreak until 982947 where another firebreak is met, wide on the right and narrow on the left. This time turn left uphill and then take the first firebreak on the right to reach a good stony forestry road (984948).

Normally walkers would wish to avoid a surface like this, but after the experience within the forest, it is a welcome sight! Turn left along it for over a mile, ignoring left and right turns. Then a clearing is reached, containing a farm building named Chartners. The track turns left, passing Chartners and climbing the hillside. The forestry road's route now coincides with the course of a bridleway shown on the map, until the forestry road turns left and the bridleway continues straight on. Very soon you are out of the forest (with relief) and into open heather moors. There are fine views of the Cheviots ahead and Tosson Hill much nearer on the right.

At this point, 994970, the route through Harwood Forest joins the alternative route round the perimeter of the plantation. The way ahead is along a delightful clear track which descends for two miles into the Coquet Valley. For much of the route it passes through heathland, but lower down there are fields and trees. After a gateway bear diagonally right on a broad green way which becomes a lane. It keeps left in front of a large dignified house, Hepple Whitefield, but it soon forsakes the house's drive and turns right along a narrow (signed) path through a clump of trees and then a field to Hepple Whitefield Farm whose access lane is followed to reach a road close to the Coquet (987 996).

Turn left along the road for half a mile. Use a corner-cutting footpath to reach the B6341 and turn right over the Coquet. Beyond the bridge take a footpath on the left which climbs to a stile on the right of a copse (981006). Turn left on the lane to West Hepple Farm; keep the main buildings on your left, then go left behind the farm, and then sharp right along a grassy track between fences. At a T-junction go left and soon turn right, round a wood. Here fine views appear of the Coquet valley and the hills beyond. The path gradually slopes left to a walkers' gate by a wood. Continue beside the wood and then go left at 970019 to enter an enormous field whose western boundary is the Coquet. Follow the eastern (right) boundary fence for a mile and then cross the river by a prominent wooden footbridge (958031). Turn left along the ensuing road and then take the first turn right into Holystone. When the village road turns sharp left (955027), go straight on along a stony track, soon turning right through fields to reach the Lady's Well. This is reputed to be 'holy', and was used for baptising Christians in Saxon times. It was positioned beside a Roman road that was abandoned long ago, so now it is secluded and surrounded by trees. The path passes right of the well and continues through fields to reach a road at Wood Hall (952037).

There is a choice of routes between here and Harbottle. The preferred way goes east along the road to 954038, then takes a bridleway north across the Coquet and through pleasant pastureland, joining the lane which leads to Harbottle Bridge (937047). But this route has a serious disadvantage, because the only way of crossing the Coquet is by wading through it, and even when it is safe to do so, walkers will get wet legs and feet, at least: stones in the river bed make barefoot crossings uncomfortable. The alternative route to Harbottle is dry but boring: just follow the road north west for a mile or so, and at the village entrance turn right to the footbridge over the Coquet.

From Harbottle Bridge, the route follows a bridleway westwards on the north bank of the river. At first it is beside the Coquet, but then it gradually rises and the river moves away so that there are good views from the path. Then the river returns and the path descends, past Park House where the surface becomes tarmac, and past a striking set of limekilns at Low Alwinton. On reaching the valley road, turn right for Alwinton.

STAGE 12: ALWINTON to INGRAM

Distance 13.1miles/21kms
Ascent 2870ft/883m

1:25,000 Maps
Outdoor Leisure 16 - Cheviot Hills

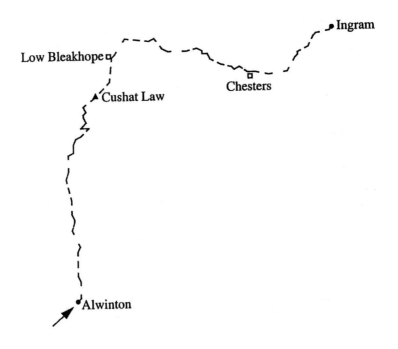

The majestic Cheviot Hills are amongst the highlights of the Northern Crossway. There is fine walking for two days in open fells with wonderful views. Farms and lanes are few. Today the main attractions are the ascent of Cushat Law (2020ft) and the delightful Breamish valley. As weather conditions can be poor, an alternative low level route is also given after the main route.

In Alwinton village green cross the footbridge over the stream and start climbing Clennell Street, a famous old drovers' road that continues into Scotland. Before long there are good views looking back along the Coquet valley. Half a mile from Alwinton, when you think that no more habitations will be seen for miles, an isolated cottage comes into view, with access through a gate from Clennell Street, which by now has become a green track amidst rounded green hills. It looks inviting, but is soon left by forking right over a stile by a gate in the fence (920074). The new path continues north, overlooking the valley of the River Alwin, parallel on the east. Suddenly a majestic view is revealed ahead, of Kidland Forest and surrounding hills, including Cushat Law. The track descends into the Alwin valley and thus unfortunately all the height gained climbing Clennell Street is lost. But on the drop to the valley, the views seem even more dramatic.

The NC follows the valley road into Kidland Forest, marked as a bridleway on the OS map. As some of the fells have not been planted, the area has an `open air' atmosphere rather than the depressing feeling of many woodlands. Occasional glimpses are seen of Cushat Law, peeping out above the trees, looking rather daunting but getting nearer each time. After 1.5 miles the valley road sheds the bridleway and crosses the river twice. Shortly afterwards bracken-clad walls on the left mark sheepfolds near the site of Memmer Kirk, an ancient valley church (922124). From here the forest road rises sharply and turns left. At its highest point turn right along another forest road whose trees have now been felled. This road climbs, turns right, and crosses a stream. Just after the stream turn left up a firebreak, climbing steeply to a stile in a fence above the treeline. Continue upward along a path and over another stile to the summit of Cushat Law. Here there is a big cairn which also serves as a windbreak. There are fine views in all directions, including Scotland and the sea.

The descent from Cushat Law to Low Bleakhope is difficult. There is no distinct path to follow, and the grass is rough and tussocky. Some paths do exist and can be used partially, but eventually lead in the wrong direction. At first go north-east without losing too much height and avoid side valleys on the left. Shill Moor opposite is a useful guide: aim for its left side. When the descent starts to get steeper, go north. Soon the farm at Low Bleakhope (935154) comes into sight. Aim for this idyllic spot in the Breamish valley.

The Ordnance Survey map shows a long bridleway following the River Breamish. In fact it is an unfenced metalled lane which serves the valley farms. For the next two miles the NC is routed along this lane eastward, and walkers can admire the attractive scenery without any problems of route finding. Gradually the lane climbs away from the river and at its highest point good views appear ahead: on a clear day you can see the East Coast. The first farm after Low Bleakhope is Alnhammoor (972154), and here the NC leaves the lane. If an escape route is needed, the lane can be followed all the way to Ingram, but it is much less attractive than the NC way.

Just before Alnhammoor go over a ladder stile on the right. Turn left past the farm and cross the bridge over Shank Burn. This stream soon joins the Breamish which has returned on the left, and the path continues through riverside fields. At 978149 it enters a plantation and climbs in earnest. It continues to rise beyond the wood and reaches the stone remnants of an ancient settlement (985149). Ahead it passes the former farm building named Chesters which seemingly had no road access. Pass between the farm building and an outbuilding which may have served as an outside privy, and follow the grassy track to a gate. Beyond the path passes eastwards through a large field full of reeds to a gate into a small wood (992147), where the path descends over uneven ground to ford a stream. The obvious path then ascends the hillside and curves round the hill amidst tall bracken. A parallel path south of this is the actual right of way but it is narrower, more uneven and boggier. The two paths combine at 998146 as a clearer track climbing over the highest point.

The climax of the day is the last mile and a half before Ingram, as the path is a beautiful green track in open hillside. The route is not quite as obvious as the map suggests, because there are several other paths and sheep tracks crossing the fell, but waymarks indicate the correct route. Eventually the track becomes stony and meets the valley road at 012161. Turn right, and then left for Ingram Bridge. The National Park Centre (refreshments) is well worth visiting: take the riverside path from the bridge. Ingram is a pleasant spot in the Breamish valley, but it is very small, with limited accommodation and virtually no public transport in the immediate vicinity.

Low Level/Bad Weather Route Alwinton to Ingram

This route includes some four miles along lanes, but these are quiet lanes where you are more likely to meet cyclists than cars. And the route starts and finishes with significant stretches of attractive paths to follow, and the gradients are moderate.

The first quarter of a mile from Alwinton coincides with the main NC route. Then at 923068 go right, over a ladder stile, along a path which crosses the River Alwin by a footbridge. Cross the cattle grid on the drive to Clennell Hall Hotel then turn immediately right, beside the hotel's boundary fence. Continue through a caravan site into open hillside (933071) and join a tractor track that rises in woodland. It becomes a fine grassy track for over half a mile, then reaches a lane near Rookland (948079).

Keep straight on along the road. For a worthwhile alternative to a quarter mile of tarmac, at 954081 take a forest track on the left into partially felled woodland. Soon fork left, then turn right onto a footpath that meanders amongst the trees. Unexpectedly there is a clearing, containing Biddlestone Chapel. This is no longer used for services, but it is intact and is open to visitors occasionally. Its access track can be used to return to the road.

In Biddlestone village go straight on beside Garden Wood, then at 963081 take a grassy track on the left. Beyond an avenue of trees turn left on a bridleway which curves right and leads to the lane above at Elilaw (977085).

Then comes the day's major stretch of road walking, from Elilaw to Prendwick via Scrainwood and Alnham. Leave the tarmac by Low Prendwick House (004125) and continue ahead through a gate on a stony track which bears right and then rises gradually. There are good views north and east, but the Cheviot heights are hidden. The path becomes a delightful unfenced green track, passing over a shoulder of Wether Hill on gentle gradients, continuing down to Ingram. On reaching tarmac (020163), continue in the same direction between the church and the National Park Centre. Take the left woodland path to Ingram Bridge.

STAGE 13: INGRAM to WOOLER

Distance 14.1miles/22.6kms
Ascent 3100ft/954m

1:25,000 Maps
Outdoor Leisure 16 - Cheviot Hills

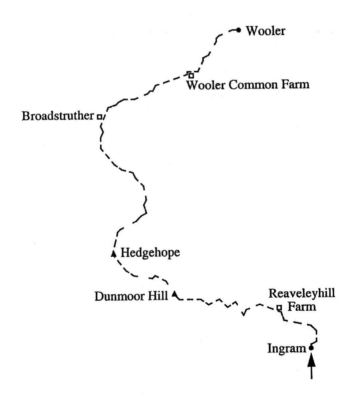

This is the climax of the Northern Crossway. As well as climbing Hedgehope Hill, the highest summit on the route, the whole day is spent in the Cheviots with spectacular views. It is the toughest day on the journey, and one that I hope will long be happily remembered. There is an alternative low level route if needed.

From Ingram Bridge take the valley road east, but turn north (left) at the first road junction. After a short half mile, take a path on the left (018171), signposted to Threestoneburn House. Immediately bear right and ascend on a rough track beside the left hand boundary for two long fields, and continue over a ladder stile into open moorland. Go diagonally right for Reaveleyhill (005178), a farm building visible on the far side of the field. From here the way is west along a green track, close but not too close to the wire fence on the right. A forest can be seen ahead - aim for its bottom left hand corner. For most of the way there is a good path. Keep right of a sheepfold, then head for a stile in the fence below the plantation corner. This is a good time to look back and savour views of the Breamish and Coquet valleys and further afield. The views get better with the climb ahead.

At this point (985181) the ascent begins in earnest. Follow a good track outside the forest. It runs beside a right hand fence to Cunyan Crags (about 1550ft) and continues up Dunmoor Hill (1860ft). Then the path loses about 300ft before crossing Dunmoor Burn, so this height has to be recovered and more climbed to reach Hedgehope's summit. There is much steady plodding up, and it gets even steeper near the top. Then at last the trig point and windbreak are reached. The wonderful views make the effort worthwhile. Hedgehope Hill at 2348ft is the second highest summit in the Cheviot range. Only the Cheviot itself (2676ft) is higher and this can be seen nearby on the west.

The most suitable way of coming down from Hedgehope is to use the path which drops steeply on the north-east side, at first close to the right boundary fence, but gradually moving away from it. The way is clearly defined and continues in a similar direction to Long Crags (956214). If you miss the way off the summit, aim for the crags which are normally visible. The path continues past Housey Crags and joins a stony path coming from the right, but soon leaves it by dropping right on a grassy path towards the Harthope valley. After three stiles, the Harthope Burn is crossed by a footbridge, and the path continues to the valley road, close beside a sheep fold (954225). If an escape route to Wooler is required at this point, turn right along this road.

The major climb of the day has been completed, but the day still has much to offer in the way of fine scenery and good tracks to follow. Leave the Harthope valley immediately by taking the path which follows the Hawsen Burn up a side valley. The first quarter-mile is unexpectedly tricky necessitating crossing the stream a few times; start on the right side of the stream. Before long the path is joined by a wide stony track that comes in on the left after fording the stream, and it continues ahead as a clear ascending track. On reaching a gate (944233), Broadstruther comes into view. This is an isolated farm surrounded by trees, and is an invaluable landmark. Recently it has been renovated, after being dilapidated for years. Continue ahead aiming for Broadstruther (941249). At a fork, where the major track turns right downhill, go straight on along a grassy track which soon curves right, gently climbing. Nearer Broadstruther turn right along a bridleway which appears to be going too far to the right but then changes direction and leads straight to the farm.

From Broadstruther the route is a well-defined bridleway, going generally north-east. As it bends right to ford a stream, take a steep path on the left to a footbridge and through a gate beyond. For the next half mile the route is along a delightful grassy path, through heather, broom and bracken, amidst attractive countryside and with a river close by. It's a shame it can't last, - but Wooler is still three long miles away. Eventually the path drops to cross the Common Burn by a footbridge (956256): for a while it stays beside the river but then it rises steadily through a wood into heather moors. Continue ahead when the bridleway is joined by a broad track suitable for vehicles.

Wooler Common is the first occupied house passed since leaving Ingram. Its name suggests that it is on the outskirts of Wooler, but it is not as close as may be hoped by walkers with tired legs! Go left beside the farm, then turn right on a broad green field track. When this forks go right, down a dip and then up over wooded Kenterdale Hill. Follow the main route through the plantation and beyond the wood bear left on a grassy track. It drops to a dry valley and reaches a rough lane by a white cottage, Waud House. Follow the lane to a road (985278) at the entrance to Wooler. Turn right along this road, Common Road, which continues as Ramsey's Lane into Wooler Market Place. Wooler is the first town of any size since Hexham and has a full range of shops and facilities.

Low Level/Bad Weather Route Ingram to Wooler
Most of this route is along quiet lanes.

Leave Ingram along the lane to Reaveley, the same way as the main NC route. But when that route leaves the lane at 018171, keep going north on the lane for almost two miles. If the hills are visible, you should get good views of Cunyan Crags and Hedgehope Hill.

At 018203 the lane curves right through trees. Leave it here by continuing straight on along a rough track that descends to cross Roddam Burn by a ford which looks rarely used. There is a footbridge on the left. The way then climbs through foliage and continues as a pleasant green unfenced track. Metalling resumes at Ilderton Moor. At a crossroads at the end of Ilderton village (017220) turn left past Cherry Tree Cottage along a stony lane. This crosses Lilburn Burn by a ford and footbridge. On the right here there is an unusual avenue of young trees: many other trees have been planted in recent years in Ilderton and Middleton, often beside the lane. The stony track ascends to meet a metalled road at 003236. Here go right and soon afterwards turn left and pass through North Middleton. The road crosses Coldgate Water by yet another ford and footbridge. Wooler is about two miles further on. It is hidden from sight until the road descends a 1 in 6 hill. It comes down Cheviot Street and continues directly to Wooler Market Place.

STAGE 14: WOOLER to BAMBURGH

Distance 18.6miles/29.8kms
Ascent 1380ft/425m

1:25,000 Maps
Explorer 340 - Holy Island & Bamburgh

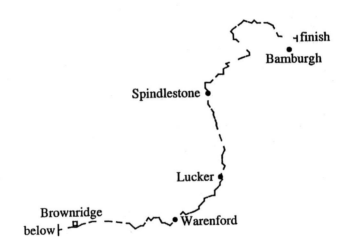

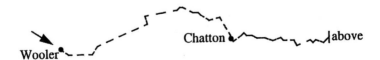

After two days in the Cheviots, there would inevitably be a feeling of anti-climax about the following day's walk, wherever it went. In fact today's walk includes several miles of fine countryside which continues until the A1 is crossed. Beyond, the prospect of finishing the walk acts as a catalyst for encouraging walkers onwards to the east coast. This stage is the longest and on most days there is little public transport in evenings from Bamburgh. So it is easier to stay in Bamburgh overnight and travel home on the following day, rather than walk all day with the pressure of having to arrive in time for the last bus.

From Wooler Market Place take the southernmost road downhill. It is named Peth Head, and later The Peth. Continue onto the A697, pass over Wooler Water, then immediately turn left onto Brewery Road which is long and straight. Eventually this road starts to climb, and swings to the right at 005279: leave it here by continuing straight on along a footpath which goes up onto Weetwood Moor. At first this is an old sunken lane but it later becomes a fine track through bracken and heather. After a cairn on the right, cross an old stone wall, but continue to walk north-east beside it, now on the left. Pass two small plantations on the left, then go down to the B6348 (026290). This is a busy road with fast cars, so take care. Turn left for a short distance before turning right onto the B6349 which is quieter.

Follow this road until it crosses the River Till. Just before Fowberry Bridge, take a footpath on the left which passes under the road by a separate arch. It continues on an old estate road of the imposing house nearby, Fowberry Tower, then turns off left into a field. Pass diagonally through the centre of the field to return to the riverbank, where it is likely to be overgrown. Make your way along the top of the embankment to a stile and shortly afterwards to a ladder stile on the right. Aim towards Henlaw Farm ahead, but curve leftwards to avoid rye grass which hides a swamp lurking beneath. Go through a gate in the top right corner and continue ahead in the next field. But then the path turns right (away from the farm) and follows field boundaries, a right hedge initially but then left after a gate. Then the track becomes enclosed between hedges and emerges onto a road into Chatton.

Chatton is a pleasant village with a shop, an inn and a village green. From the green go down Church Hill, then left on Old Road, past Chatton First school. Rejoin the B6348, cross the River Till, then take the second lane on the right. This is a metalled no-through lane, over a mile long to Shielhope farm (082281). Just as the farm is approached, fork right through a gate to join a track shown as a white road on the map. It is three miles long and was constructed in 1872 for a visit by the then Prince of Wales to Chillingham Castle. Proceed left on this 'road' for a very short distance to a collection of gates and animal pens: go through the right hand gate and follow the field boundary which rises to a gate in the far corner. The path, now with a fence on the left, levels out around Coalhouses (087281) - a name on the map denoting a former building, now just rubble. Continue generally eastward, amidst undergrowth when fording Coalhouses Burn.

Beyond the burn pass through a waymarked gate. Go left through bracken to meet a fence which consists of a single thread of barbed wire. Turn right beside this fence, following it when it curves left, but now on a clearer path, for about a quarter of a mile to 092283. Here at a path junction turn right uphill and then immediately fork left to go eastwards through the moorland. The broad grassy track passes right of Brownridge Plantation and then goes round a ruined farm, Brownridge (100283). Beyond a gate here, go diagonally left via a stile to another gate. The path now goes east for a mile, initially along the boundary of Brownridge Plantation but then aiming for a gap between two plantations. A modern barn is in front of the right hand plantation: as the path passes the barn (116285) it becomes a forest track. Carry on along this, fording two streams. After the second ford the track becomes a metalled road, catering for the farm and cottages at Twizell (127287).

The busy A1 trunk road is half a mile away from here, and its traffic noise is clearly audible. Turn right beyond Twizell on a footpath signed "Warenford 3/4 mile". It immediately goes left as a good stony track, then forks right in the wood. Its route thereafter is not easy to describe as it twists and turns in the woodland, and there are also several private tracks. Fortunately the right of way is well waymarked, so follow the waymarks and be guided by the noise of the A1. Eventually a track wide enough for vehicles is reached at 133286. Follow this under the new A1 to reach the old A1 in Warenford village. There is an inn nearby.

Warenford marks the boundary between moorland and farmland. The hills have been left behind, and now all that's left is the final eight miles of the journey to the east coast. If you wish to halt at this point, Warenford is on a bus route. To carry on eastward, cross the old A1 and take the lane to Lucker opposite. Go through a walkers' gate on the right into a long field and cross the Waren Burn in the far right corner by a wooden bridge. Continue on the track uphill. When a hedge is reached (142286) turn left beside it. At a clearing (146285) turn left between trees along an overgrown lane that hasn't seen a wheeled vehicle for years. At first this is not easy walking, but eventually the way becomes easier to follow: nevertheless it is still a relief to reach a tarmac road (153293) which is followed left into Lucker, where there is an inn.

The way forward from Lucker is north-east along the riverside path which is mostly in the adjacent field. It returns to the Waren Burn in order to cross the main line railway; the path is on an unusual metal bridge under the railway yet directly above the river (156307). From here the path continues to a stile in the top corner of the field. Cross a road here and carry on in the same direction along a boundary for two fields to a farm at Bradford (152323). Pass between the farm buildings and continue ahead through a small field with the hedge on the right of the path, followed by a larger field with the hedge on the left. In the far corner drop steeply in a wood to two bridges over streams. Climb out into a field, and meet a road at Spindlestone (150333).

Turn left along the road, descending to an old mill by the river. Here turn right along a minor road, but soon (149337) take a footpath on the right uphill, signposted to Drawkiln Hill. The path is clearly marked through woodland and fields, then briefly enters Waren Caravan Park. Here turn right beside the hedge and reach a lane (156340). Turn left up the lane which swings right by the caravan site entrance and then reaches a road at a T-junction. From here the sea is visible at last! Go left along the road, ignoring tempting side paths, going gradually downhill.

On reaching the B1342 turn right, then immediately take a footpath on the left going diagonally right through the field to a ladder stile in the far corner. Cross, then turn right beside the fence. The path descends to a mobile homes colony (160355); here turn left along a tarmac bridleway. After Heather Cottages take a path parallel to the coast, but behind the sand dunes and the remnants of wartime coastal defences. The path becomes clearer and emerges onto a shelf with a fine view overlooking the estuary, a pier nearby and Holy Island in the distance. It continues, curving round the headland and Bamburgh Castle comes into view. The end of the trek is in sight! Further east, the path follows blue posts to the Club House of Bamburgh Castle Golf Club. Here there are some bungalows and a metalled road. The castle is the dominant feature of the landscape and it looks more majestic as it gets nearer.

Follow the road to the start of Bamburgh's built-up area. After passing '30mph' signs and 'The Boat House' on the left, turn left on a rough track and left again along a footpath towards the castle. It joins a clear way from beach to village: turn right to a large village green and keep on its left beside the castle. Beyond the green, keep going along an upward path which is positively the last climb of the NC. It curves left and meets the public entrance to the castle. Reach the gate house - a pair of round towers with an archway in between - and touch the stonework to complete the Northern Crossway.

TRANSPORT

To Arnside

Arnside is on the Lancaster to Barrow-in-Furness railway line and it is best approached by train from Lancaster. There is a regular service on weekdays but a less frequent service on Sundays.

From Bamburgh

The nearest station to Bamburgh is Berwick-upon-Tweed which has a good service on the East Coast main line. There is a reasonable bus service from Bamburgh to Berwick (sometimes requiring a change at Belford) on weekdays, but a limited service on Sundays. South of Bamburgh, buses tend to go to Alnwick from where a bus to Newcastle-upon-Tyne can be taken. But these services are limited, especially on Sundays, so although Newcastle is particularly well served by trains, it is probably easier to travel via Berwick.